The GLOOMSTER

Text from 'Der Verdrüßliche' by Ludwig Bechstein

First published in Germany in 2010
by Jacoby Stuart
First published in the UK in 2011
by Faber and Faber Limited
Bloomsbury House, 74–77 Great Russell Street,
London WC1B 3DA

Printed in England by Butler, Tanner and Dennis Ltd, Frome, Somerset

A CIP record for this book
is available from the British Library

ISBN 978-0-571-27424-6

2 4 6 8 10 9 7 5 3 1

Ludwig Bechstein

The GLOOMSTER

or Terribly Gloomy

Illustrated by Axel Scheffler
Translated by Julia Donaldson

ff

faber and faber

I'm feeling gloomy.

When I feel gloomy
It makes me feel gloomy.

Sunshine is dazzling,

Birdsong is frazzling,

Wine is too sour for me,

Beer's not my cup of tea,

Honey's too sugary !

Everything turns out wrong.
That's why, the whole day long,
I feel so gloomy.

Music depresses me.

Dancing distresses me.

People who have their fling
Fill me with suffering.

All of it drives me mad !

All of it makes me sad,
Makes me feel gloomy,
Terribly gloomy.

Even more maddening
Is that black shadow thing.

Why must it follow me?
Why can't it let me be?

Clouds are another curse,
Making me feel much worse.

Winter is cold and drear,

Spring comes too soon each year,

Summer is much too warm,

Midges in Autumn swarm—

On my hands, overhead,
On the walls, round the bed!

Oh how they irritate!
How they infuriate!

Heartburn! Vexation!
Hell and damnation!

Nothing is right for me.
Turn out the light for me.

Let me be gloomy,
Terribly gloomy.

The Gloomster

I'm feeling gloomy.

When I feel gloomy
It makes me feel gloomy.

Sunshine is dazzling,
Birdsong is frazzling,
Wine is too sour for me,
Beer's not my cup of tea,
Honey's too sugary!
Everything turns out wrong.
That's why, the whole day long,
I feel so gloomy.

Music depresses me.
Dancing distresses me.
People who have their fling
Fill me with suffering.
All of it drives me mad!
All of it makes me sad,
Makes me feel gloomy,
Terribly gloomy.

Even more maddening
Is that black shadow thing.
Why must it follow me?
Why can't it let me be?
Clouds are another curse,
Making me feel much worse.
Winter is cold and drear,
Spring comes too soon each year,
Summer is much too warm,
Midges in Autumn swarm –
On my hands, overhead,
On the walls, round the bed!
Oh how they irritate!
How they infuriate!
Heartburn! Vexation!
Hell and damnation!

Nothing is right for me.
Turn out the light for me.
Let me be gloomy,
Terribly gloomy.

Der Verdrüßliche

Ich bin verdrüßlich!
Weil ich verdrüßlich bin,
Bin ich verdrüßlich.

Sonne scheint gar zu hell,
Vogel schreit gar zu grell,
Wein ist zu sauer mir,
Zu bitter ist das Bier,
Honig zu süßlich!

Weil nichts nach meinem Sinn,
Weil ich verdrüßlich bin,
Bin ich verdrüßlich.

Dort wird Musik gemacht,
Dort wird getanzt, gelacht,
Dort wirft man gar den Hut,
Wie mich das ärgern tut!

Ist nicht ersprießlich,
Ist nicht nach meinem Sinn,
Weil ich verdrüßlich bin,
Ach, so verdrüßlich.

Wo ich auch geh und steh,
Ich meinen Schatten seh,
Immer verfolgt er mich,
Ist das nicht ärgerlich?
Und wenn der Himmel trüb,
Ist es mir auch nicht lieb.

Winter ist mir zu kalt,
Frühling kommt mir zu bald,
Sommer ist mir zu warm,
Herbst bringt den Mückenschwarm.
Mücken auf jeder Hand,
Mücken an jeder Wand.

Oh, wie mich das ergrimmt!
Oh, wie das mich verstimmt!
Wie das ins Herz mich brennt!
Himmelkreuzelement!

Bin ganz verdrüßlich,
Weil nichts nach meinem Sinn,
Weil ich verdrüßlich bin,
Ach, wie verdrüßlich!

Ludwig Bechstein (1801–1860) was a German writer, librarian and archivist. In his lifetime his patriotic poetry and historical fiction were widely read. Today he is chiefly remembered for his collections of fairytales and legends.